COUNTING WITH HARLEY

1 2 3 4

By Jennifer Logan

Illustrated By Maruf Hasan

To order additional copies of this book, contact:
Xlibris
1-800-455-039
www.xlibris.com.au
Orders@Xlibris.com.au

ISBN: Softcover   978-1-7960-0649-0
       EBook   978-1-7960-0650-6

Print information available on the last page

Rev. date: 09/18/2019

COUNTING WITH HARLEY

Jennifer Logan

"Good morning Farmer Matt."
"Good morning Harley," replied Farmer Matt.
"Are you going to count today, Harley?"
"Yes! Farmer Matt. I have just counted one farmer."
There is one farmer.

"Bye Farmer Matt," Harley called out as he
trotted to a nearby field to find some farm animals to count.
"Hello!" Harley said to the sheep.
Harley counted the sheep one..two.
There are two sheep.

Harley came across the farmer's working dogs, Maple, Wyatt and Blue. They were all having a rest before going to work. Harley counted one..two..three. There are three dogs.

Harley looked over the fence and
counted..one..two..three..four pigs
having fun in the mud.
There are four pigs.

"Hello Harley" said Daisy. "Are
you having fun counting all the animals?"
"Oh Yes!" replied Harley.
"I love counting." Harley counted the cows..
one..two..three..four..five..
There are five cows.

Harley came across the Goat family going
for a walk. "How many goats are there?"
thought Harley.
I will count them.
one..two..three..four..five..six.
There are six goats.

The ducks are so happy to see Harley.
"Are you going to count us today, Harley?"
Mother duck asked.
"Yes" replied Harley. "I will count out aloud
so you all can count with me."
All the ducks counted with Harley
one..two..three..four..five..six..seven.
There are seven ducks.

Harley noticed the hens out in the field so he galloped over to count them one..two..three..four..five..six..seven..eight. There are eight hens.

8

"Do you want to play with us Harley?" asked the rabbits.
"I would love to, but my Mother is calling me so I only
have time to count how many rabbits there are." replied Harley.
Harley counted the rabbits
one..two..three..four..five..six..seven..eight..nine.
There are nine rabbits.

"Have you had fun today Harley?" asked his Mother.
"Yes! Thank you Mother. I have counted the animals on the farm.
I only need to count all the horses now and I will be finished."
Harley counted the horses
one..two..three..four..five..six..seven..eight..nine..ten.
There are ten horses.

Printed in the United States
By Bookmasters